# THE MANY MOODS
# OF DIS-EASE

## Who I Am As I Am

Ross Worcester Best Putnam

# PRAISE FOR *THE MANY MOODS OF DIS-EASE*

Ross's work is reflective, honest and earnest. His poetry gives voice to the heart of a person who is in a constant state of discovery and exploration of a world he now faces and has not chosen. His work speaks of the power and courage we all hold in our heart and the common thread of uncertainty we share. The poems are reflective glimpses into one man's experiences of hope, obstacles, strength, fear and charm. *Patrick LoSasso, Parkinson's Community Advocate, Personal Trainer*

Ross is a "mad poet" offering his poignant, powerful words to the world through the lens of Parkinson's and his own unique life journey. Taking a disease that can drive one mad with frustration, disappointment, confusion, and loss and creating beauty from it. He brings it all forth – spirit and soul, humor, the wonderings, insight and power. A great gift. *Dru Phoenix, Counselor, Art Therapist and Spiritual Healer*

Ross's art of poetry, and drawings of his life have been discovered through his personal adventures with living consciously as embodied mind and soul. Ross tells the path of his journey laid out from Discovery, through the byways of Despair, Compassion, Acceptance, Transformation, Healing, Hopeful, and Gratitude. All the while, showing us each a grand invitation for our own self examination and expression of whole, holy, wholeness. Truly, his uniqueness becomes a beacon of light for us all. *Jules, Friend (with an artistic soul), Master Mystic (for the hands and feet of self-discovery)*

With the very "generosity of heart" of which he writes, Ross Putnam offers his thoughts as he lives with Parkinson's Disease. Speaking in an intimate tone, he seeks the essence of his experience and takes the reader with him to its spiritual heart. *Sally Buffington, writer and photographer*

I am one who is not afflicted with Parkinson's Disease, as Ross is. I have known Ross for over 60 years and am acquainted with his gifts of deep caring and of expressive language. I have greatly appreciated his previous book *An April Shower of Poems*. In his new book, Ross skillfully draws me into his situation and helps me walk his walk with him. This is the gift he shares with all who read and ponder the experience of living with Parkinson's Disease. *J. Donald Schultz, MD*

Ross is a man of grace, courage, inspiration and humility. His inner strength is reflected in the honesty, candidness and authenticity in which he writes. In this beautiful book of poems, he offers us a poignant and open view of his life experiences. Ross creatively navigates his emotional experiences of traversing life with Parkinson's while creatively weaving us through the eight stages of his living with his disease. He refuses to allow any physical limitations of his body to restrict the expression of his inner soul and spirit. He reminds us that we are all merely spiritual beings having a human experience. *Dr. Kris Brew, Chiropractor*

To one whose career was devoted to providing pastoral care to people working their way through the crises of everyday life, Ross's poems remind me of those personal pastoral encounters. In "The Doctor Visit," "Choices," "Walking the Mountain," "Until," in poem after poem, we encounter a person dealing with a sensitive issue, not in some esoteric language that leaves us confused, but in words we understand. In these poems, I keep thinking I see Ross, entreating us to be brave and hopeful and determined, and at the same time I see Ross with a smile and a twinkle in his eye, urging us to relax. *The Reverend Mr. Jack Merner, a country boy, Yale Divinity School graduate, father, grandfather, now having reached the age of 100. I take pleasure in praising the work of a good poet!*

With poetry as his pallet, the author creatively draws us into the brush strokes of his life as a person with Parkinson's. Living with a disease now recognized as more complex than any other, Mr. Putnam creatively gifts the reader with a glimpse into the myriad moments that make up life with Parkinson's. Whether or not disease has touched your life, I highly recommend *The Many Moods of Dis-Ease*, and encourage you to take Ross up on his offer to "walk with me". In doing so, you just may create the opportunity to discover your "own unique being". *Nancy D. Floodberg, MS, President – San Diego Central County Parkinson's Support Group, Board Certified School Neuropsychologist, ret.*

Outskirts Press, Inc.
http://www.outskirtspress.com

Paperback ISBN: 978-1-9772-3527-5
Hardback ISBN: 978-1-9772-3804-7

Cover and Interior Design by Drea Caruso, Graphic Designer
© 2021 Ross Worcester Best Putnam.
All rights reserved - used with permission.

Outskirts Press and the "OP" logo are trademarks belonging to Outskirts Press, Inc.

PRINTED IN THE UNITED STATES OF AMERICA

# PREFACE

I have a book of pictures of Vermont which looks as if they were taken some time in the nineteenth century. In one of the photographs a farmer is pitching hay onto a horse drawn hay wagon as ominous clouds billow overhead. The caption reads: "Think it's going to rain, Grandma?" Turning the page reveals a photo of an ancient, wise woman. This caption reads, "It'll be a long dry spell if it don't."

Making predictions is a risky business in the world of weather and about any field one can imagine. And yet we humans continue trying.

There are times when it seems the less we know about something, the more eager we are to say what we believe is coming next. My experience with Parkinson's disease is a case in point. As much as is known regarding the inevitable outcome of this progressive, degenerative disease, no one can tell anyone what the journey will be like. There are no charts or graphs which will tell anyone what the speed of the process, the pain, the impact, the physical, emotional, relational, spiritual, or financial costs will be.

I hold that as good news. It gives me a foundation from which I can search for hope. The poems herein have been gathered together in shared themes and emotions. That some of the poems could easily fit under multiple headings speaks to the mindset each of us has at any particular time.

So read on! It is my hope that this book offers you the opportunity to discover much about yourself, those for whom you care, or life in general, allowing for grace and joy to emerge in the midst of the journey you and they travel in this life of Dis-Ease.

## THE MANY MOODS

## WE ARE ONE

We are one in spirit and soul
So it has always been

We share a history, experiences and discoveries
We've talked at every turn

Now – suddenly – with no warning comes the diagnosis
So unlike anything we dreamed

Questions rage – we are befuddled
So unlike what would or should or could befall us

At first dawn after that day of shock
Comes numbness, a sense of doubt

Yet still, a light burns brightly
Of hope to shield us from the unknown

# AT THIS AGE

At first
The diagnosis staggered me – though not for long
Too young to have "it," – too young to be defeated

Now, years later
Still too vibrant to be demoralized
Still too enlivened to surrender

What I expect
    What I want
        What I need
            At this age

To walk more slowly
To see more clearly
To act more patiently

        What I need
      What I want
   What I expect
At this age

Is a generosity of heart for myself
Acceptance of who I am now
A belief that I am not alone

# MARKERS

Mile markers of life, we call them
    Easy to document, rejoice or lament upon

The newborn advances
    Learning new skills, gaining more understanding

And elders decline
    Stumbling along, slipping in memory

Not as easy in my case
    Each person is unique, their own special blend

The markers others accomplish I might not
    They tell a story, not necessarily mine

I invite you to walk with me
    To celebrate my markers

If they fall outside the norm
    That will be all right

They testify to who I am as I am
    My own unique being

## IMPERFECTIONS

There are standards across the spectrum
We demand perfection in everything
Clothes, cars, houses, jobs and food
Anything not up to the best it could be
Is worthy of rejection

We live in a flawed world
Homeless, ill, lonely, lost and diseased
They are amongst us
Not worthy of rejection

In the end we all have imperfections
If we would accept each other as we truly are
If we could help one another
If, if and if again

## YOU DON'T KNOW ME

So much of what can't be seen in me today
Is wrapped in the shroud of the person
    I was
    Or may have been
    Becoming

I will not revisit those reminders
What – but for misplaced application
    My past is mine
    Only I can carve
    Comfort from it

You cannot know me now by
Pontificating, guessing or speculating
    I emerged from the
    Who, what and how of yesterday
    Only I have that key

Every new today of my life
Evolves and blossoms into
    The me of now

## DARK NIGHT

Dark soul in the night
Not sleeping again
I rattle through hallways of
    Where I've been
        What I knew
            What I used to do
                Where I dreamed of going


In the pitch of night
Stalking corridors known a while ago
Now filled with
    Sinister shadows
        Foreboding symbols
            Ominous signs
                Mystifying memories


In the midst of this night
Robbing me of sleep
I grasp for a knowing
    That will not haunt me
        That will guide me
            That will comfort me
                That will shield me

## THE DOCTOR VISIT

"Show me how well you walk
Without a cane"
                    "I use the cane for safety," I reply

"Push yourself
Challenge yourself
Test yourself"
                    "Or use caution?" I ask

Right now I feel propelled to walk
A few steps
        Unaided
                Are worth
                        The effort

# FORMULA

Drugs, tinctures, timing
Which drugs, what dosage, what schedule?

Everyone is guessing
No one knows

They struggle with the formula
I struggle with the results

In fact, there is no single path
As I follow mine, I'll find my way

# EMOTIONS

An aching brain, shattered ego or bruised heart
Is susceptible to
    Blame, guilt and anger
    Rage, shame and anguish

A wounded body, injured soul or crushed spirit
Is vulnerable to
    Narrowing options and vanishing resources
    Pessimistic thoughts and imagined hurts

A lost hope, defeated effort or failed attempt
Is foundational to
    Despair and discouragement
    Worry, dread and terror

Even so – dreams remain
Though wind blown and flickering
    A jubilant moment emerges
    Brief, fleeting, even in the darkest hour

Come
Hold my heart
Guide my spirit
Move with me away from the edge

## THE HONEST TRUTH

I am angry
    On my way to a secure, joy-filled future
    A sign I had never acknowledged asserted itself
    "Your arm should swing matching your step"

"Really? I had no idea," I was baffled
    Medical diagnosis confirmed the worst
    My living in casual dismissal is at an end
    So fast, so simple, so cruel

I'd rather a lover reject me
    Or lose my favorite possession
    Or break my every bone
    At least I could do something

But this disease
    How does it pillage me?
    How can I live now?
    Why should I live now?

This disease is gestating in me
    Its iron grip constricts me
    I am mystified, confused, disoriented
    Is there no negotiation? No bargaining? No postponing?

I am angry
    I was on my way! Doing well
    Now I'm a stranger even to myself
    Foundations solid yesterday, crumble now

My carefully groomed hopes are torn asunder
    Because of this mind-robbing, resource-embezzling,
    hope-skimming disease
    Lumps me with people I shuddered and ignored
    Any control I ever pretended to usurp has vanished

The reality I have aspired to make mine
    The lenses through which I see
    The voices with which I plea
    Now elude my use and torment me

My balance barely saves me, at the crumbling precipice I stand
    I must adjust and adapt
    I cannot shrink back in terror forever
    I need to face the new reality of me

Hold me until I find and love my new self

# THEY SAY BUT I'M THINKING

"We admire you"
    I'm counting mistakes I made today

"You look so much better than last we saw you"
    I'm scared

"Where do you get your strength?"
    I focus on my falls

"What gives you the courage you display?"
    I'm worried

"You're looking good – walking tall and boldly"
    I'm exhausted

So many say such wonderful things
Yet I balk at the affirmations

Is it denial to not believe the positivity?
Is what they say the real me?

How can I accept the truth that is?
How can I let it take hold of my heart?

## THE COLD

Who has the password for my supply of energy?
The vault has been cleaned out
What endurance I had is bankrupt

Who authorized the hijacking of my resources?
Are the makers of remedies conspiring?
The symptoms overcome all defenses

Eyes weighing five pounds pull the lids down
Sniffles, sneezes, aches, and pains
Even the mightiest kneel to the "Porcelain Throne"

All I care about is getting healthy

## FIGHTING SEPARATENESS

How much easier it would be
When I'm tired or ill at ease
To hide till the coast is clear

Yet another side of me knows
Without the world
I'm gathering dust

With little purpose

## DON'T TALK ABOUT ME

Now I understand the ill and the ancient
I know they once were young with dreams
And why they now don't want to be seen

Now I stutter and slur
Yesterday I talked effortlessly
Now I move with stumbling hesitation
Yesterday I walked without thinking

Now I imagine you talk about me
Be gentle
I'm human

# I'M DONE

Mind over matter perhaps
More care with each step
I'm done

Broken bones, scrapes, bruises
Take forever to heal
I'm done

If falling comes to my door
I shall ignore its knocking
I'm done

# Compassion

# EMPATHY

A stranger jumps to open the door where I point my cane
    "Take your time
    No rush
    Watch your step"

Another time laden with grocery bags
    "Do you need help?
    Are you alright?
    What can I do?"

Losing my balance an arm reaches to catch me
    "Take my hand
    Let me help you
    It's my pleasure"

These exchanges flail at my
    Pride
    Self-pity and
    Arrogance

Their tender touches moisten my cheeks with tears
    Their concern strengthens me
    Helps me re-frame my reality
    I see, reach for, begin to believe
    I can unlatch a door to my future

# MY FALSE FACE

I am so very transparent
    My gait stumbles and catches
It sometimes helps to say out loud
    "It's Parkinson's Disease"
It sometimes helps to hear
    "I'm here for you, I've got you"

I am so very private
    You'll not see me seethe
It sometimes helps to throw a cane
    As if it were the cause
It sometimes helps to hear
    The clatter of its metal on floor

I am so very aware
    How I present makes a difference
It sometimes helps to say
    "I'm fine," when I am not
It sometimes helps to hear
    The declaration that affirms

I am so very intimate
    This disease and I are one
It sometimes helps to be quiet
    To listen to the silence
It sometimes helps to hear
    The tranquility of nothing

## LET ME HELP YOU

There's something about having a strong arm beside me
To catch me before a fall
Or help me when I am down

I used to be that arm
Confident in my perception
Able in my ability

Now, not swift of foot nor stable support
I need not sit idly by
Feeling pity for self and unhelpful to others

I know I can be strong in others ways
Offering an encouraging word, a thoughtful smile
Being an advocate and friend for those in need

## TOUCH ME

Touch me
>    Do not be afraid of my crooked body
Reach for me
>    My stutter-step need not embarrass you

This disease will do much
>    Slow, stiffen, slur

It will
>    Invade my body
It will
>    Corrupt my mind

This disease will do much
>    Isolate, irritate, interfere

It will not
>    Lessen my love for you
It will not
>    Lessen what I can learn

Touch me
>    With your caress comes connection
Reach for me
>    With your embrace comes divine healing

## THE NAP

I want to be productive – to add to the value of life
    But I'm so tired

"Take a nap if you need to," she says
    But that costs time I do not own and cannot control

"Take a nap and rest, no worries," she says
    But time cannot be recycled – it's gone

"Take a nap," she says, "rejoice that you can"
    Finally I believe her – as my eyelids,
    Lubricated by her compassion slide shut

# IN THE SAME ROOM

I want to avoid the room with others like me
    We who share the same disease
    Are not the same

We have a code, though rarely do we speak of it
    When in the same room
    We dance around the awkwardness

Lest by broaching the realities we become them
    Less able – more vulnerable
    Less permanent – more unstable

Of course, what I miss then, is refreshing grace
    Showered on me – blessing me
    With their help for me – my help for them

I'd rather be ignorant of other's ailments – or so I thought
    So today I dare to say, "Introduce me to all in the room
    I will gain even as we wane"

# Acceptance

# THE SCOOTER

As my legs more frequently failed me
I found a new way to traverse the world

A mobility scooter: Atto, by name
She folds, buzzes and toots

With lights, throttle – she'll carry a load
She's cool, well designed and noticed by all

Atto transports me and stokes my liberated self
Comments, questions and envy shower me like ticker-tape

Riding her, old boundaries collapse my caution and reluctance
I plow on – up and down hills with excitement

For independence, adventure and thrills I am grateful
Free as a bird at dawn's refreshing light

As free, and even fun, as Atto is
Truth be told, I'd rather be walking

## EXCUSES FOR THE MIND TO MELT

The causes are many
    chemicals
        trauma
            fear


The receptivity to healing is dependent on much
    availability
        agility
            age

In the end, it is mine
    whatever the cause or reasons
        whatever the state of things

It is my decision
    to live more fully
        to become more open

## CHOICES

There is a lot at stake
We have to decide our approach
    We will be informed
    We will weigh the risks

We need a carefully prescribed plan
That outlines the many options
    Emotions will not hinder or restrain
    Doubt will not be welcomed

How do I care for my life
My well-being is at stake
    Experimental trials and meds
    Testing which diet works best

I need to do what I have to do
I am the one who choses my path
    I may not be in control of my body
    I am, for now, in control of my decisions

It is my choice

## ALMOST HOME

You'd think they'd know
>These engineers, designers and workers
>To be my friend this scooter must function

I would wish them to know
>A gauge is a gauge
>Exactly how much power is left?

It shouldn't happen
>But it did – almost home
>Battery ran dry

As if by plan, a man walking dogs
>Happened by
>"Let me help you," he said

Embarrassed,
>I steered, he pushed
>Two blocks to my home

Relieved and grateful
>No words suffice
>My helper disappeared out of sight

## SIX MONTHS LATER

No worry on my mind
Till suddenly without warning

Atto, the scooter, just stops
Same street, same corner

As if by plan, a man walking dogs
Was there again

Same man once more
"Let me help you," he said

"No more reunions," we both agreed
"At least not this kind!"

## VOICE

I've found my voice in verse
Now to use my verse in voice

And speak with intent
And truth

## HOURS IN THE DAY

You cannot get ahead of time
Rather than be buried in the dust hurrying creates
Slow down, dear heart

You are called to live only now
Rather than take responsibility for all time
Slow down, dear one

You are able to see what emerges
Rather than cloud creation with busyness
Slow down, dear love

You are allowed to receive this day's balm
Rather than run ragged all the time
Slow down, dear breath

# AT SOME POINT

There comes a point of
Asking, "What's the point of living?"

I am going to die
    From, with, because of
        Or even
            In spite of
                This disease

I am going to die
    Neither this disease
        Nor the absence of it
            Will spare me
                The finality of life

I long to know the answer
    Not how or when
        But the best tact,
            Approach or attitude
                To apply to living now

## TRUST THE CAT

Cats have the right idea
    If you're tired, sleep

No second thoughts
    No guilt or hesitation

Snuggled into a pillow
    Cuddled into a person

This is my new approach
    If I'm tired, I'll sleep

## WALKING THE MOUNTAIN

It's the view, we are told
It's just around the corner, we are promised
Apply yourself, stretch yourself, push yourself
We are urged

So we climb on
In spite of thorny branches, loose footing, scraped knees
We rest with increasing frequency
Yet we move onward

So we go on
Through the storms and setbacks
The blinding sun on cloudless days
Reminded of the goal's beauty and inspiration, we climb higher

The mountain has many peaks and valleys
What one calls the pinnacle is for another only a foretaste
There seems always one higher experience, vantage,
Goal to reach

My mountain, come to find out
Has lower, rounded summits
One roles into the shoulder of the next which appears higher,
If only slightly

Here I rest to consider what I've been told
"Leave the higher places to others"

# Transformation

## STAYING TUNED

Do I choose rowing, walking, or boxing,
Yoga, chi gong, or tai chi?

The options are many but the story's the same
If I miss a day it's time lost

If an hour is good, surely two will do more
To build up, develop and strengthen my core

So I'm on the lookout every day
To find, learn and strengthen another way

# CHRYSALIS

What surrounds me I cannot see
    Restricting movement hampers me
    I want to burst the unknown constraints

Within those limits lies transformation
    The invitation is to surrender
    To the coming change of new life

Words have yet to be discovered
    To fully tell me what is to come
    I dwell in uncertain hope

That chrysalis, my chrysalis,
    Is to be my home, my haven
    Till the day I embrace my new being

How long it will take I cannot tell
    No longer a caterpillar, not yet a butterfly
    I resist the transformation

I hang here more comfortable now
    I wonder what lies ahead
    I open myself to the unfolding

## NEEDLESS FEAR

I panicked when my trusty scooter
Atto quit; just up and died

My mind leapt to catastrophe
Cars bearing down

I was pride-wounded only
Danger was exaggerated

I got out of the way
I made it home

There's enough fear already
No need to generate more

## MY SILLY CANE

My silly folding cane has a mind of its own
I swear

It has taken as it's holy calling to keep me guessing
I'm sure

This piece of worked metal hides at hurried times
It's clear

I'm sent scouring my memory to find it again
I know I'm near

It has a quick smile and ready grip
When it finds me

## YOU MAY DISAGREE

You may think I'm crazy
You may disagree with me
    What I think and feel

Be careful what you say
You don't know my state of being
    Why I chose this path

None of us knows the truth
Keep the light shining
    As we move forward
    Into Mystery

# UNTIL

Our fate is not cast upon us
We are not pawns
Helpless
Hapless
Hopeless

The Divine within us
Is ours to
Discover
Develop
Devise

We, You and I
Every person
All resources
Are Co-Creators
With all that is Holy
For all is Holy

Until we see each other as extension of ourselves
Until we apply whoever we are and have and hope to be
To every dream and limitation
Until we accept, love, respect and nurture
Every person, culture and belief

Diseases, problems, issues, and hindrances
Will continue to plague and restrict us
And Pogo will be right:
"We have met the enemy
And it is us"

## ANOTHER MOMENT

As I'm tossed by chance and plan alike
The "to do" list is longer than I thought
    I'll never finish now
        I better get moving
            Oh my gosh, look at the time

As I deal with necessities we like and dread
Somethings will have to wait
    There's so much to do
        I'll get to priorities first – tomorrow
          I really have to go now

As another moment passes by
Ticked away on the clock of life
    Now I question, wonder and worry
        Did I use that tick well and fully?
        Let me live as if I did

As I sit in the dusk of the day
There's much I've consigned to tomorrow
    The day has been full
        To find love, purpose, dream and call
        I'll embrace each moment

## CELEBRATING THE PRESENT

In my glance of daily news
I am caught unawares
A photograph reveals a young girl dancing
Exhilarated in the joy of the moment

Around her is squalor
The refugee camp
Bespeaks the horror of war and uncertainty
This is her home, all she has

Her jubilance displays the power of hope
The innocence of youth
The fear of yesterday has passed
The terror of later today is not yet upon her

I am transformed by her triumphal essence
Her courage inspires me
She fills my heart with assurance and promise
I will join her in the celebration of the present

# Healing

# OASIS

I cannot name the forces
    I cannot identify them
        I cannot see where or when

Realities, coincidences, fortunes
    Clash
        Conspire

Suddenly I'm snared in their grip
    Uncertain
        Unknowing

Fear permeates my every breath
    Scared
        Shaking

The oasis I so desperately need vanishes
    Ripped
        Torn

Confusion takes hold of my being
    Fear
        Irrationality

I need to keep seeking
    I need to accept
        I need to believe

The Oasis will be there

# THE HEALING HAS BEGUN

Exhausted from aches, pains and embarrassing glances
Collected while navigating the now gone day

Sitting on bed's edge urging my reluctant legs
To move under the warm comforter

My plea is that they allow the renewing,
Refreshing sleep I so need to soothe my troubled body

As night's shadows soften the sharp images
Of the day's frustrations pounding my head

Then without announcement or explanation
A knowing, a clear sense, a confident assertion filled my being

Words burst into my soul: "The healing has begun"

They lathered my soul and loosened the shackles
Which had limited my day
In that instant I glowed
    The mystery
        Limbered my legs,
            Feet and toes

As if to punctuate the truth I then knew
My newly empowered feet
In one smooth move
    Were now warmly,
        Tenderly, gently, welcomed
            Under consoling covers

It made no sense, of course
Contrary to medical science,
No empirical evidence, just the sensation
    Challenged assumptions
        Wafted through my hopeful mind
            Scurrying for how to respond

Will the knowing continue in days to come?
Perhaps
Who knows?
    It happened in that moment
        I sank into the joy of it
            For now I live with new hope

# SURVIVING

When the shaking earth unhinges all things stable
When flames consume all we are and have and want
When the unfathomable disease destroys all things certain

Little else matters
Loss takes on new meaning
Leisure is unknown

I forgot how to laugh
I forgot how to smile
I forgot how to care

Simply surviving is all that's left to me
Grab whatever smatterings of sanity I can
Despair consumes me

In the exhausted quiet of stagnation
If I would unclamp my petrified eye lids
I would see the dawn of reality

Life is mystery
Manageable if we celebrate who we are
Instead of where we were

Come talk with me
We'll teach each other to laugh again
And learn together how to thrive

## THE INVITATION

I invite you
    To believe
        No God hunches over a control panel
        Running our lives
        No sweaty finger holds us over Hell's fire
I welcome you
    To believe
        The presence of a holiness
        Awaits to be absorbed from all there is
        Accepting, encouraging, understanding
I challenge you
    To believe
        No matter our wanton ways or anguish
        The sacred presence comes as pure light
        Absorbing, extricating, comforting
I dare you
    To trust
        No matter how forgotten or alone
        Pure light flows as love to one another
        Inexhaustible, undefinable, invincible
I tempt you
    To trust
        Divine energy gives assurance, comfort and healing
        Take my hand and we will discover
        Release, renewal, repose
I encourage you
    To trust

# CURE(D)

Headed home after a wonderful trip
Nervous worry floods my mind
I feast on adrenaline supplied
By a tight, anxiety-filled schedule

Standing on the curb, waiting for a rideshare
My mobility scooter won't fold completely
Sweat blurs my eyes
Time pulsing by stokes the fires of my panic

Finally the rideshare arrives
The driver relaxes tension with friendly chatter
With ingenuity and patience
The scooter is nestled in the trunk all better

My cane and I settle into the front seat
We're on our way to the airport
For the moment all is well
Then the words from the radio jar my mind

I ask the driver,
"What's that we're listening to?"
And he says,
"It's a Christian radio talk show"

I never know what to say to that
Why did I open my mouth?

Then he wants to know,
"What's going on with your body?"
"Parkinson's," I say
Knowing it's a conversation stopper

His next words surprise me,
"I'd like to pray for you"
"Fine," I say
Knowing it would never work

At the drop off, he prays
Bold and confident he demands I be cured

Will I be twenty-five again?
Vital, healthy and wise?
His parting words,
"Do that which was difficult – you'll be able to"

His words – my questions
Shape the journey from now on
His belief – my hope
Breathe possibility into my spirit

# THE CENTER OF MY LIFE

Why do I turn
A blind eye
A cold heart
A closed mind
To others in need?

Self-care takes center stage
    Remind me to broaden my circle of interest

Self-care can become self-absorption
    Remind me to widen my heart's perspective

Self-care without interest in others becomes selfishness
    Remind me to welcome others into my heart

Self-care needs balance
    Remind me I am part of a larger whole

Hopeful

# SOURCE OF HOPE

Locked in forgotten chambers of the mind
    Be it wishes, hopes and dreams
        Solutions, desires and sensations

Plant them deeply in the soil of your memory
    Rooted, attainable, accessible
        They are there holding hope

Tend them gently, use them often
    Solving challenges, regrets and wounds
        Embossing images, sounds and wisdom

For when the time comes and you are alone
    If nothing else
        Hope will feed you

As nothing else can

## IF

If only I had started earlier
If only I had exercised more
If only I had used the cardio machine

Who knows?
The time is now
Not then

I am where I am – who I am as I am
I am glad for that
I am glad for this day

# ANGER

Anger is the crabgrass in our garden of life
    It chokes out beauty
    It hides nurturing light
    It gulps the water

Anger stymies great, inspired plans
    It blinds us from pleasantness
    It crimps our hands
    It drains our energy

Anger must be faced
    No matter the depth of its roots
    No matter how effectively we use it
    No matter our justification

Anger is a pathway
    Not a dead-end street
    Not an endless source of misery
    Not without hope

Anger can be an avenue to wholeness
    If we face it
    If we ask for help
    If we trust ourselves

# FINGERS

My fingers spent much of the day
Hesitating, balking, cramping
They chased the cursor around the screen

Scattering misspellings across the page
Typing invented words making no sense
Draining my brain, wanting escape and relief

Twisted, gnarled, afraid to move
I rub, shake and curse fingers
That only yesterday worked fine

My heartfelt desire is to stop
Take it up another day
I can find something less agonizing to do

Yet as corrosive anxiety is dispersed
Creative words and thoughts erupt
I am torn between abandoning and persevering

Sufficient hope remains
To calm my fears and journey boldly
To a new tomorrow

## INTRICACY

There is nothing so delicate as a spider's web
As it shimmers in the day's early light
Holding droplets of dew

The sun pierces the tiny beads of moisture
Emblazing them for a moment into dazzling chandeliers
Lighting and brightening the day

There is nothing so intricate as its pattern
The expanse of design flawless in its perfection
An invitation to pause and notice

The humble spider spins its time away pleasing our senses
As pressing needs and troubling worries weigh us down
May we create beauty as our own legacy

## REFLECTION

I know for some, God is a conversationalist
    A constant companion
        A guide for every step, every decision, every choice

My God is not a receiver of bribes nor promises
    No matter how good the cause
        Rather, a listener to all
My God is not a distributor of blessings nor curses
    No matter how great the need
        Rather, a presence to be sought
My God is not a manipulator of tides nor storms
    No matter how tragic the loss
        Rather, a strengthener of grace and love
My God is not an inflictor of disease nor pain
    No matter how well deserved
        Rather an inspirer of verse and voice
My God is not an entrepreneur selling privilege nor advantage
    No matter how rich the asker
        Rather a challenger at every stage

My God is reflective
    Being seen in the eyes of another
        Being heard in the kind words of another
            Being felt in the gentle touch of another
My God is everywhere
    Being seen in the majesty of flowing rivers
        Being heard in aspen wood's summer breeze
            Being felt in the possibility of a new tomorrow

# DRUMS

Behind the chaos
    Beneath the fear
        Beyond the uncertainty

A heart-beat is drumming from earth's soul
    Listen for its pulsing
        Feel its vibration

Slow your pace
    Step reverently
        Stop – Be still

The drum's rhythm reverberates from the sky
    It calls your attention
        It can sooth your furrowed brow

It comes with strength and wisdom
    From the heart of the universe to your very own
        It will support you as it has from time's beginning

## HOW ARE YOU?

The challenge is to find answers – not depressing words
I want to tell, of course, what is different
What's different is what I notice
What I notice is what doesn't work as well
What doesn't work as well as before

Ah, there's the rub
Which words, gestures, expressions do I use?
"Relax," I say to myself before speaking
It will come
That is my core belief
And my hope

## THIS MORNING

I awakened knowing
    Challenges lay ahead

I awakened optimistic
    To embrace the day

I awakened eager
    For the opportunities at hand

## I WISH

If I could make a difference
Beyond the ordinary, every day

Time runs away like rain on the sidewalk
Before it can be harnessed fully

I wish I could change the current of life
In fact I do make a difference

# Gratitude

## LIFE LINE

Her first thought when we met
    "I want to spend the rest of my life with you"
    I wanted to marry her!

I speak of this now for
    She lives in the shadows
    Overlooked, under-noticed

I call on this now because
    She is my life line
    Responsible at each turn

She keeps me afloat
    Her endurance astounds
    Her strength abounds

She needs to be celebrated
    It cries out to be said
    I give thanks for my wife

## LOVE

Love and care
Concern and interest
Come from everywhere

Love and care
Concern and interest
Carve fear from my heart

Loving care
Concerning interest
Make me feel for the moment

For this moment
Love is real

## IT'S THE LITTLE THINGS

A kind word softens my heart and lifts my spirit
Intended for me or not
     I have co-opted it for my needs

You have given me a moment's glistening peace
You have touched the depths of me
     Your gentle smile reminds me I am loved

In that fleeting exchange my eyes open to this new day
I am grounded in joy and strengthened in mind
     My spirit soars in the wind

## ARNIE

I knew Arnie only by watching him deliver the daily newspaper
Hard not to see him as he flew on his bike
    Smoothly down the street
        Sack on his back bulging with rolled print
            Announcing the latest happenings from near and far

My young mind admired his dependable dedication
Nothing could dissuade him from his appointed rounds
    Artfully swinging into driveways
        Tossing the papers onto our porch
            Off again, doing his part to keep us informed

With no explanation, all I knew – he was gone
Arnie, what was so wrong that you had no options?
    When and how did joy leave you?
        What robbed you of hope?
        What signs did we miss?

Now these years later I recall his ready smile
    Dodging all obstacles to remain alert and on schedule
        Cool, attentive, in control
            I envied his endurance and agility

I am thankful for the reminder
    To ask when I am low
        To give when others despair
            To trust in a hope for a better tomorrow

## THE FOURTH

Easy conversation and a shared meal
A quiet evening anticipating the annual spectacle
 High on a hill
 Almost out of hearing range

Situating chairs to best capture the view
A refreshing evening with cherished friends
 Delighting in the glow of the setting sun
 Recognizing the gifts of each one

Spectacular colors, sizes and shapes bursting above
Every offering celebrated shared memories
 We are one together
 With and because of our diversity

I came away with a spring in my step
Taller, perhaps
 At least in my mind
 At least for that moment

I give thanks for being swept away from symptoms
Will it make a difference tomorrow?
 It makes a difference now
 Celebrate the now

# IN THIS TOGETHER

The reason I breathed life's dawn today
    You may not know
The reason I unlatched hope's door today
    You cannot tell
The reason I'm not overwhelmed is you

Every night, every day you teach my heart to love
    Though at times I may not show it
You taught me to be open to both joy and pain
    Though I often resist
You taught me the reason to live at all

When I can no longer lead with my right
    Or stand up at all
When I can barely remember my name
    Or speak for what I believe
My struggle wears thin against your love

This disease is a disease for both of us
    We are partners
Together we build on all we have been
    Discovering life along the way
We are adventurous, resourceful and resilient

Together we live *The Many Moods of Dis-Ease*

## ACKNOWLEDGEMENTS

From my early years I have dabbled in writing poetry. As the years passed I became more interested and serious in my writing, especially when a friend challenged me to write a poem a day during April, National Poetry Month. I accepted that challenge. Then with more encouragement I published a book of those poems, *An April Shower of Poems*, complemented by several of my original drawings.

Once that was accomplished I was inspired to create a journal in poetry form focusing on the many trials and travails, as well as the blessings and revelations of living with Parkinson's Disease. It has been a rollercoaster ride of emotions that I have come to learn that most encounter as they also live with many neurologically degenerative diseases.

In this book I expose myself to the world while confessing to the many emotions and moods one daily finds themselves encapsulated in, even momentarily. I offer these poems in hopes of reaching others, inviting them to find themselves recognized, known and supported throughout those times when life seems more anguish and misery than upbeat and joyous.

I owe a deep gratitude to the many people who read my first book and encouraged me to write this one. To all those, thank you! To members in the poetry groups I met with monthly while writing many of these poems, I am appreciative of your words of praise as well as correction.

A heartfelt nod of gratefulness to friends and family as they supported me these many years and months giving space and time in their lives reading and otherwise helping this book come to fruition.

In particular I pour out my love and thankfulness to Drea Caruso, graphic designer extraordinaire, and motivational cheerleader with a generous heart of gold who toiled for many hours bringing this book to life.

Lastly, I acknowledge my partner and wife, Paula Jean Elizabeth. Her affirmation, determination, insights, and love have guided me throughout the development and publishing of this book.

For all named and unnamed, for all the love and caring, for all the tedious work and long hours, I am grateful for the outcome and for each of you.


## AUTHOR

Ross Worcester Best Putnam was conceived, born, raised and was a member of the community of Lyme, New Hampshire for his first eighteen years. He was inspired by the originality, creativity, and resourcefulness of his parents, siblings, and town folk through the vicissitudes and triumphs of life.

He earned an A.A. from Multnomah Jr. College (Oregon), a B.A. from Heidelberg College (Ohio), an M.Div. from Earlham School of Religion (Indiana), and an M.A. from Southwestern College (New Mexico).

His interest in art, writing in general, and poetry in particular, has been honed over many years. He is the author of *An April Shower of Poems*, a book of poems for each day of April, National Poetry Month. He lives in San Diego, California with his wife, Paula Jean Elizabeth.

CPSIA information can be obtained
at www.ICGtesting.com
Printed in the USA
FSHW021951041121
86004FS

9 781977 235275